HANDLING
the
SWORD
of
DELIVERANCE

DR. D. K. OLUKOYA

Handling The

SWORD *of* DELIVERANCE

◆ DR. D.K OLUKOYA ◆

© 2012 A.D.
HANDLING THE SWORD OF DELIVERANCE
Dr. D.K. Olukoya
ISBN: **978-0692489215**

A Publication of

TRACTS AND PUBLICATIONS GROUP
MOUNTAIN OF FIRE AND MIRACLES MINISTRIES
13, Olasimbo Street, off Olumo Road,
(By UNILAG Second Gate), Onike, Iwaya.
P.O.Box 2990, Sabo, Yaba, Lagos, Nigeria. 01-867439, 4704267,4704367
Website: www.mountainoffire.org
E-mail: mfmhqworldwide@mountainoffire.org

I salute my wonderful wife, Pastor Shade, for her invaluable support in the ministry. I appreciate her unquantifiable support in the book ministry as the Cover designer, Art editor, and Art advisor.

Contents

CHAPTER 1

ARROWS *of* DELIVERANCE

ARROWS OF DELIVERANCE

In this book, we are considering a very important topic which has raised a lot of controversies among Christians. It is the topic of deliverance. We would start with the arrows of deliverance. I advise you to take advantage of this message and learn how to shoot the arrows of deliverance.

2 Kings 2: 11-14 says:

> *And it came to pass, as they still went on, and talked, that, behold, there appeared a chariot of fire, and horses of fire and parted them both asunder, and Elijah went up by a whirlwind into heaven. And Elisha saw it,*

> *and he cried, My father, my father the chariot of Israel and the horsemen thereof. And he saw him no more; and he took hold of his own clothes and rent them in two pieces. He took up also the mantle of Elijah that fell from him and went back, and stood by the bank of Jordan and he took the mantle of Elijah that fell from him and smote the waters and said, Where is the Lord, God of Elijah? And when he also had smitten the waters, they parted hither and thither and Elisha went over.*

2 Kings 13:14 says:

> *Now Elisha was fallen sick of his sickness whereof he died, and Joash the king of Israel came down unto him and wept over his face and said, O my father, my father, the chariot of Israel and the horsemen thereof.*

Joash king of Israel was a very young man and inexperienced. The Syrians were after him and he was weak. He knew that he was weak. Any time the

Syrians were attacking him and his people, he was very fortunate to have Elisha at home. He would always run to him and say, "Daddy, they have come." And Elisha would say, "Just go to that corner and you would capture them," and he was having an easy run. By the time Elisha was 80 years old and was about to die, the king began to cry and say, "My father, the chariot of Israel and the horsemen thereof." But Elisha had no words to waste.

2 Kings 13: 15-16 says:

> *And Elisha said unto him, Take bow and arrows, and he took unto him bow and arrows. And he said to the king of Israel, Put thine hand upon the bow. And he put his hand upon it: and Elisha put his hands upon the king's hands.*

The hands of the king of Israel were shaking vigorously. He was weeping not because Elisha was dying, but because he too might die because the Syrian soldiers would kill him. He was a pathetic character. Something happened to him that changed all that, Elisha put his hand upon the shaking hands of the king. God will do that for you today, in the mighty name of Jesus.

No matter how confused and terrible things are going, all you need is His hands upon your own hands. Is your business not moving the way you think? Just lay His hands upon your hands.

Verses 17-18 say:

&& *And he said, Open the window eastward. And he opened it. Then Elisha said, Shoot. And he shot. And he said, The arrow of the Lord's deliverance, and the arrow of deliverance from Syria; for thou shalt smite the Syrians in Aphek, till thou have consumed them. And he said, Take the arrows. And he took them. And he said unto the king of Israel, Smite upon the ground. And he smote thrice and stayed. And the man of God was wroth with him and said, Thou should have smitten five or six times; then hadst thou smitten Syria till thou hadst consumed it: whereas now, thou shalt smite Syria but thrice.* ""

He had God's arrows in his hands but did not use them well. Elisha shouted when his master, Elijah was being carried away, "My father, my father, the chariots of Israel and the horsemen thereof." Joash too, said to Elisha, "My father my father, the chariot of Israel."

WHO WAS ELIJAH?

Elijah was a wonderful prophet of God for several reasons:

1. Nothing is known about his parentage. This teaches us that we do not have to be important before God can use us.

2. He was the first prophet to announce that there would be drought and famine.

3. He was also the first prophet God used to multiply food.

4. A careful study of the Bible reveals that he was the first prophet to raise the dead.

5. He was the first prophet to close up heaven and put the key in his pocket.

6. He was the first prophet to pray for immediate rain and it fell.

7. He was also the first prophet to call down fire that everybody could see.

8. He was the first prophet to write a death letter to a king (2 Chronicles 21:12-15).

9. Elijah, by his counsel, example, prayer power and boldness, did more to preserve Israel than the whole army of Israel put together. He was a one-man army.

10. Elijah left a good example for people after him to follow.

What would you be remembered for when you die? Would it be said that you are the one that prevented so many people from getting born again? A lot of people are popular for doing evil things today. But Elisha was not like that. He got a double portion anointing from his master while Gehazi who could have got the four portions got leprosy instead. Why? Because he was covetous.

THE DIFFERENCE BETWEEN ELISHA AND JOASH

When King Joash knew that Elisha was about to die, he was crying instead of collecting the anointing. Elisha shouted at him to take the appropriate step. Herein lies the big difference. Elisha passed his own assignment, but Joash failed. There is, therefore, serious danger in saying the right thing halfheartedly or allowing depression, anger and worry to get you down because in that situation, although you have arrows and have been told to fire, you will not be able to do enough work. The arrows of God will never miss, they will strike when they are fired. That king could have done better, but he was not bold. So, he did a very poor job. God loves people who put everything into what they have to do.

The type of Christianity that does not teach you how to fire the arrow of deliverance is mere religion. When the early Christians came to Nigeria, they could not make much impact; apart from establishing schools and teaching people how to read and write. They did not understand the spiritual.

It is a known fact that many Christians are lazy; and lazy people are useless in spiritual warfare. The devil would use every slackness in the life of a person to gain advantage. Maybe, you are wondering and asking: "Why me? What have I done to deserve all these? How can God watch as bad things happen to me? What is going to happen?" You need to understand a little bit about the ministry of deliverance.

Luke 4:18-19 says, "The Spirit of the Lord is upon me because He hath anointed me to preach the gospel to the poor; He hath sent me to heal the brokenhearted. To preach deliverance to the captives and recovering of sight to the blind, to set at liberty them that are bruised. To preach the acceptable year of the Lord."

A portion of the above passage says, "To preach deliverance to the captives."

PRAYER POINTS

1. O Lord, guide me into the mysteries of my life, in the name of Jesus.
2. Let the eyes of the wicked monitoring my life be darkened, in the name of Jesus.
3. Every power assigned to wreck my destiny, you are a liar, die, in the name of Jesus.
4. O God, arise, and confound my enemies, in the name of Jesus.
5. Circle of confusion, break, in the name of Jesus.
6. Terminators of my father's house, die, in the name of Jesus.
7. Thou vagabond power assigned against me, die, in name of Jesus.

CHAPTER 2

What is
DELIVERANCE?

WHAT IS
DELIVERANCE?

Deliverance is expelling bad spirits that torment or protect people. That is why Jesus said, "In my name, shall they cast out devils." Evil spirits are of different categories. Some are babies while others are adults. Some have experience while others are not too experienced. When an experienced demon is harassing a person, you have to be strong to cast it out. Some demons, when you tell them to get out, in the name of Jesus, would say, "We have gone." Then you begin to wonder, if they have gone, why are they still talking?

A man of God said to a demon, "You demon of nicotine, get out of the life of this man, in Jesus' name." And the demon said, "I have gone." Then the man of God said, "If you have gone, why are you still talking?" The demon then said, "Stupid man, I went out and I came in again." The man of God said, "How did you do that?" It said, "I went out through one route and got in through another." This meant that there were so many routes in the life of the man upon whom he was ministering deliverance.

I visited a friend of mine and she told me that her daughter was not doing well. I talked to the daughter and we started praying. Suddenly, something lifted her from the chair, slammed her on the floor and she began to swim on the floor like a fish. When I said, "You foul spirit, get out of her, in the name of Jesus," a male voice from her answered and said, "Leave her for me, she is mine, leave her for me, she is mine." Then her mother screamed, "Yea, I have been reading about these things in books but I never knew it could happen in my own sitting room, and to my daughter too." There are so many demons hiding in many lives and if you do not challenge them, they would muster all available weapons to prevent their victim's escape. But when there is a serious challenge, they have no option than to come out. This is why sometimes, when some people pray aggressive prayers, that is when they would have the worst dreams. Why? Because, maybe for the first time in their lives, their swords have touched blood.

2. Deliverance is to loose the bands of wickedness.

There are so many bands of wickedness trailing so many lives. Sometime ago, some people were serving pounded yam somewhere and one brother calculated that by the time they would get to him, the portion he would get would be the smallest. So, he decided to pull a fast one. He called the man who was to take the biggest portion and said, "Excuse me, somebody is calling you outside." As the man went out, he grabbed his food and began to eat. When he came back and saw the brother eating his food, he was angry and placed a curse on him and right from that day, anytime the brother sat down to read his books, it would seem as if somebody was pounding yam on his head. If he did not try to read any book, there would be no problem. But if he attempted to read, the pounding would start. He ran to a place for prayer and they told him that his grandmother was responsible for his problem. He knew they were not saying the truth because the person who was responsible threatened him openly. He went to another place and they said, "You don't need deliverance. You have been set free." But by the time he got home, the pounding started again. What was happening to him is what we call the bands of wickedness. Breaking that is what is known as deliverance.

A lot of people just walk into trouble. For example, I have never seen anyone being dragged to the disco hall by force. Everyone that goes there does so willingly. Disco halls are usually not well lit, and people collect all kinds of evil load from there. It is the same thing with pepper soup joints. A man told a woman, "Madam I am taking you out for lunch." And the woman was excited. She thought they were going to a five-star hotel. When they got to the place which was built with wood, one fat woman that was sweating profusely came out with a bucket and said, "Yes, you are here for pepper soup, point to the fish you want inside that bucket so that we can prepare it for you immediately." Anyone that has patronised such places needs deliverance.

3. Deliverance is also to destroy the yoke of the enemy.

A yoke is something you use to join two animals together. If one is fast and the other is slow, the slow one will slow down the fast one. Deliverance is to break that yoke so that you can move forward. A certain brother did not know why things were not working well for him until he prayed and the Lord said to him, "Go to your grandmother, your life is in her hands." He went there and said, "Mama, I have come to collect my life," and the mama said, "So, you have been told. Go under the bed, and bring that bottle." Under the grandmother's bed were bottles for all his brothers and sisters. He asked her what was in the bottle and she said, "I was the one that took your delivery when you were born and I cleaned the blood and water off your body. The water and blood are inside the bottle and that is what I have been using to control you. But since you have found out, you can take your bottle." That was deliverance. We had a case where a sister who was set free from the demonic world brought a big broom and I asked her what it was used for. She said, "Simple, when I don't want a woman to stay in her husband's house, I sweep her out of the place with this one." Deliverance is to destroy that kind of thing.

4. Deliverance is to break curses and spells that have been put upon people.

There are some families where majority of the women are not married and even those that are married are having serious problems building their homes. Such people need deliverance to be free from such bondage. There are some families, where the curse of poverty is in operation and anyone that tries to prosper just dies suddenly. I know of a brother who was travelling to his village every weekend. I tried in vain to warn him about the inherent dangers, more so when he did not have the Holy Spirit baptism. He was going into the domain of the enemy without the necessary power to fight with. Eventually, he was buried inside his uncompleted house.

5. **Deliverance is freedom from forces of oppression.**

For example, alcoholism, unnatural sexual urge, bedwetting, masturbation, false religion, etc. Deliverance is needed from all these. If an aggressive prayer point is called and you notice a strange movement in your body or anytime you smell incense or hear the sound of drums, you get excited, deliverance is needed to break the forces responsible.

6. Deliverance is the spiritual cleansing of a place.

It is the chasing out of bad spirits from a house, office, shop etc. and destroying the satanic decrees upon them. There was a brother who used to sell things. Initially, he used to have a lot of customers but suddenly, he noticed that they stopped coming to his shop and were buying from the shops around him. One day, he saw one of his best customers buying things from another shop and he called him and said, "Excuse me, you used to buy things from my shop, why are you now abandoning the place?" The customer replied, "I don't know. I just don't feel like coming there." Then the man started to pray and God gave him a revelation. It happened that all those surrounding him had been meeting at night. They took sand from the front of his shop to somewhere, did something to it and returned it. And because most of the customers were not born again Christians, they were easily influenced. But after he prayed and anointed the place with anointing oil, that satanic embargo was broken.

7. Deliverance is blocking of satanic holes.

Some people are in these kinds of holes. It is like someone who is inside the prison and his wife serves him delicious meals three times everyday. He can be eating all those things but the fact still remains that he is in prison, he is not free. Some people, when they are quarrelling with others, say all kinds of things without the power to back them up. Some would say, "You cannot do anything, my blood is bitter." The person saying that his or her blood is bitter may be committing fornication. That fornication will then help the enemy to put sugar in his blood and it will become sweet in the mouth of witches. A woman of 42 told another woman she was quarrelling with, "I go show you say woman pass woman." And she did not have any power to back up that statement. Before she knew it, she began to bed-wet. In fact, it got so bad that she was using nappies. Even though she was a leader in one church, they still dealt with her. It was after she went through deliverance that her bladder was healed.

8. Deliverance is the removal of invisible heavy loads placed on people.

The prayer point that says, "All the owners of evil load, carry your load, in Jesus' name," is a serious one.

9. Deliverance is uprooting evil seeds and evil trees planted in a person's life.

Sometimes during deliverance, you find people vomiting live snakes and different kinds of things. What were the snakes doing in their bodies and how did they find their way there? Evil seeds have been planted there.

10. The enemy roughens the journey of people, but deliverance makes it smooth.

11. Deliverance is a destruction of the works of the devil.

12. Deliverance is the removal of satanic embargo placed on the lives and ways of people.

Deliverance will help you to spoil all those that have been spoiling you and deal with all those that have been robbing you. There are many methods of deliverance but the best is what I call, 'praying it through.' Therefore, I would like you to fire some arrows before you read further.

PRAYER POINTS

1. Every anti-breakthrough device against my life, be shattered to irreparable pieces, in the name of Jesus.
2. I paralyze every satanic attack from the womb, in the name of Jesus.
3. I paralyze every evil leg walking about for my sake, in the name of Jesus.
4. Let all the evil blood that have mingled with my blood be drained out, in Jesus' name.
5. I break every evil unity organized against me, in the name of Jesus.
6. No dark meeting held on my behalf shall prosper, in the name of Jesus.

7.   Let the backbone of the strongman and the stubborn pursuer break, in Jesus' name.

8.   I refuse to allow my angels of blessing to depart, in the name of Jesus.

9.   I cancel the effect of any bad name upon my life, in Jesus' name.

10. I paralyze all aggression addressed to my star, in the name of Jesus.

11. Lord, bring honey out of the rock for me, in the name of Jesus.

12. O Lord, open all the good doors of my life that household wickedness have shut, in Jesus' name.

13. I neutralize all the problems originating from the mistakes of my parents, in the name of Jesus

14. Circle of confusion in my life, break, in the name of Jesus.

CHAPTER 3

The SWORD *of* DELIVERANCE

W e would start this chapter by considering Judges 7:16-23. This is the story of Gideon.

" *And he divided the three hundred men into three companies and he put a trumpet in every man's hand with empty pitchers and lamps within the pitchers. And he said unto them, Look on me and do likewise and behold when I come to the outside of the camp, it shall be that as I do, so shall ye do. When I blow with a trumpet, I and all that are with me, then blow ye the trumpets also on every side of all the camp and say, The sword of the Lord and of Gideon. So, Gideon and the hundred men that were with him, came unto the outside of the camp in the beginning of the middle watch, and they had but newly set the watch: and they blew the trumpets and brake the pitchers that were in their hands. And the three companies blew the trumpets, and brake the pitchers and held the lamps in their left hands, and the trumpets in their right hands to blow withal; and they cried, The sword of the Lord, and of Gideon. And they stood every man in his place round about the camp: and all the host ran, and cried,*

> *and fled. And the three hundred blew the trumpets and the Lord set every man's sword against his fellow, even throughout all the host: and the host fled to Bethshittah in Zererath and to the border of Abemeholah unto Tabbath. And the men of Israel gathered themselves together out of Naphtali, and out of Asher, and out of all Manasseh, and pursued after the Midianites*

The book of Judges is a fantastic book to read. You would notice that in it, God was put at the last position while human beings put themselves at the first position and generally, when things are organized that way, problems inevitably come. So, because of this ungodly arrangement, problems started and the children of Israel were suffering. The suffering was so much that after they planted and were about to reap the harvest, their enemies, the Midianites, would come and take away everything. It got so bad that they were afraid to prepare food for the fear of being harrassed. At a time, Gideon was somewhere, trying to prepare some amount of food and was hiding to do it for the fear of the enemy. While he was busy doing this, the angel of God

26

stood by and said, "The Lord is with thee, thou mighty man of valour." Gideon said, "Angel, don't deceive me. Which peace are you talking about? Don't you see what I am doing here? I am hiding here because if they find me, I will be in trouble. Where are all the miracles our fathers recorded?" The angel said, "Okay, so, you are wise. Go in this your might and deliver Israel." That was how Gideon took over the mantle of delivering his people from the oppression of the Midianites. Here, you see him in one of his favourite battles where the sword was used. There were two swords: the sword of the Lord and that of Gideon and when the sword of the Lord came out, the enemies cried, ran, and started to fight themselves with their own sword. So shall it be for your enemies, in the name of Jesus.

The sword as a weapon of warfare has won so many battles. Through the sword, men have created and destroyed empires. The sword has also been used for aggressive warfare and for protection.

Let us do a small Bible study on the sword of the Bible so that you can understand what I am saying better. In the garden of Eden, Adam and Eve misbehaved. They disobeyed God and God drove them out of the garden. And God did something in Genesis 3: 24:

> " So he drove out the man; and he placed at the east of the garden of Eden Cherubims, and a flaming sword which turned every way to keep the way of the tree of life. "

Adam and Eve were driven out of the garden, and an angel protected it with an interesting sword which the Bible calls a "Flaming sword that turned every way."

A brother was living in a very demonized house. When he moved into that house, there were two demonic priests living there. The first thing he noticed was that the two demonic priests were quarrelling over customers. One would be accusing the other of taking over his customers. So, they fought and eventually, the more powerful one won, and the other one ran out of the house, leaving the stronger one and the brother. So, the one that was left switched his fighting gear to this brother, he complained about his vigils and mode of prayers. However, the brother refused to stop praying, and war started. One night, this demonic priest turned into something else and went into the brother's room. When he got there, he saw the greatest film show of his life! Surrounding the brother was a sword of fire turning in every direction. He was so amazed that he stood there and watched the brother till dawn, while the brother was snoring away; not knowing that there was somebody there wanting to destroy him. The demonic priest had no choice than to bow to the power of God. He was forced to confess to the brother what he wanted to do and narrated what he saw in his room that night.

Deuteronomy 32: 39 - 42 says,

" *See now that I, even I, am he and there is no god with me. I kill, and I make alive; I wound, and I heal: neither is there any that can deliver out of my hand. For I lift up my hand to heaven, and say, I live forever. If I whet my glittering sword and mine hand take hold on judgement; I will render vengeance to mine enemies and will reward them that hate me. I will make mine arrows drunk with blood and my sword shall devour flesh; and that with the blood of the slain and of the captives, from the beginning of revenges upon the enemy.* "

This passage is telling us that God has His own sword, whose functions are:

1.   To render vengeance to His enemies,
2.   To reward those that hate Him and
3.   To devour the flesh of the enemy.

Take note that we have seen two types of swords

now - the flaming sword in the Garden of Eden and the glittering sword mentioned in the passage above.

Joshua 5:13-14 says,

" *And it came to pass, when Joshua was by Jericho, that he lifted up his eyes and looked and behold, there stood a man over against him with his sword drawn in his hand; and Joshua went unto him, and said unto him, Art thou for us, or for our adversaries? And he said, Nay; but as captain of the host of the Lord am I now come. And Joshua fell on his face to the earth, and did worship, and said unto him, What saith my Lord unto his servant?* "

So, we have the sword of the captain of the host of the Lord drawn out; it is the sword of victory. If you are ready to use this sword then pray this prayer point: "The Lord of host, draw your sword against my adversaries, in the name of Jesus."

In Jeremiah 47:6, we see this empty appeal to the sword of the Lord:

> " *O thou sword of the Lord, how long will it be ere thou be quiet? Put up thyself into thy scabbard, rest, and be still."* And what was the answer? Verse 7 says, *"How can it be quiet, seeing that the Lord hath given it a charge against Ashkelon, and against the sea shore? there hath he appointed it.* "

God had given the sword an instruction. When the Lord appoints His sword, none can stop it and the sword of the Lord will not keep quiet until it has destroyed the adversary. It does not matter what kind of appeal is made to it like the empty appeal seen in Jeremiah 47:6 above. The sword of the Lord will not keep quiet until it has destroyed your adversaries, in the name of Jesus.

The enemy, satan is far from being gentle and it is a time-wasting exercise being gentle with him. The only language he understands is force. If roasting the devil is not sufficient to make him release his captives, then bomb him. The important thing is to be free.

Revelation 1:16 says:

> *And he had in his right hand seven stars: and out of his mouth went a sharp twoedged sword: and his countenance was as the sun shineth in his strength.*

Revelation 2:16 also says:

> *Repent; or else I will come unto thee quickly, and will fight against them with the sword of my mouth."*
> See also Revelation 19:15: *"And out of his mouth goeth a sharp sword, that with it he should smite the nations: and he shall rule them with a rod of iron: and he treadeth the winepress of the fierceness and wrath of Almighty God.*

This is the sword of the Lord Jesus Christ, coming out of His mouth and so, shall your enemies be smitten with it, in the name of Jesus.

From the foregoing, you can see that the sword is an important spiritual tool.

CHAPTER 4

How to use the SWORD and what to use it against

HOW TO USE THE SWORD AND
WHAT TO USE IT AGAINST

The sword of deliverance must be used in aggression, both to protect yourself and to fight the enemy. The sword must be used against:

1. **The devil:** The Bible calls the devil a restless destroyer. We know that the devil has power, but his power is limited. The only person with limitless power is the Lord Jesus Christ, because He says, "All authority and all power in heaven and on earth have been given unto me." The devil has never said that before. If he had all power in heaven, it would not have been possible to throw him down. He is a restless destroyer. Demons do not go to bed. They are busy prowling, seeking whom to destroy. In the book of Job, we are told that the devil moves to and fro and up and down. 1 Peter 5:8 says that he walks about like a roaring lion seeking whom he may devour.

Somebody said that by talking about deliverance, one is glorifying the devil. This is not true for if we ask the demon of the river to get out of a person's life and it goes out, who is that glorifying? Is it the devil or God? Or did Jesus not say, "If I, by the Spirit of God can cast out devil, then the kingdom of God has come unto you." So, deliverance is part of what is in the kingdom of God.

My finding is that many pastors are scared of talking about evil spirits. They are afraid the evil spirits will descend on them back at home. This is not true unless there is no fire in the minister. Satan is a restless destroyer and you do not defeat him by treating him with kid's gloves. Moses, the Bible says, spoke to God face to face. Yet those magicians were so bold, they wanted to compete with somebody who has spoken to God face to face. Who gave them that confidence? The devil. When he threw his rod down, they said, "Oh, that's easy; we can do that as well." So, they threw their own rods down and the rods turned into snakes. Moses said, "Okay, if this is how you people are going to play the game, I command your river to become blood," and it did. So the magicians said, "No problem, we also can do that." So, the rest of the water that people should have been drinking, they turned it into blood. Moses said, "Okay, I will bring out frogs," and he did, and frogs were jumping everywhere and the people said, "No problem, we can do that as well." They brought out frogs. Then Moses said, "Okay, let there be lice on man, animals, trees, everywhere." Lice started. To bring out simple things like lice, they tried but could not, then one of them said, "This is the finger of God. Let us leave them alone and let them go." Which power did these magicians use in performing the magic? The power of the devil. So, he has some power but it is limited.

2 **The flesh:** The second thing you should use your sword against is the flesh. It has killed so many people. The flesh has destroyed more than all the witches and wizards put together. It is the flesh that is responsible for statements such as, "They are annoying my spirit, they are calling me names, they are gossiping about me," etc.

One day, I was going out with a brother and some people about a 100 meters away were chatting. This brother then said to me, "Dr. Olukoya, those people are gossiping about me." I did not believe he could hear what the two gentlemen were saying, so I ran to them to find out what they were saying and discovered that they were talking about a football match. The flesh.

Terrible habits like bleaching, wearing of false nails, nose-piercing etc, all with a view to making you "look beautiful" is the result of uncrucified flesh. One major syndrome that has killed many in our environment is, "This is how they do it." And because many have not dealt with the flesh, they too do it and run into trouble.

I have had cause to challenge many to show me where it is written in the Bible that people must have bridesmaids and best man or even wear wedding gowns during their weddings. Where is it written that you must borrow money to rent a video man to cover your wedding? It is really amazing to see some men exhibiting their chests with big chains. It is nothing but the work of the flesh. You have to use your sword to kill this flesh.

3. The world: You are to use your sword against the world. The world system in which we find ourselves is a place we do not belong for our citizenship, the Bible says, is in heaven. We operate under a different law from that which the world operates.

4. **Principalities:** You use your sword of deliverance against principalities, that is, strange spirits walking about. You use your sword of deliverance against evil authorities, evil dominions and against the rulers of darkness. As soldiers of Christ, we are meant to be terrorising and harassing them, and not the other way round. They worry Christians instead of Christians giving them sleepless nights. This is rather unfortunate.

A lot of families are under evil domination. A single witch in a family could become a source of problem to every member of that family. You are to use your sword of deliverance against such a witch. This sword should be used against evil thrones. There are many things that are reigning as kings around. You may have a boss in the office who bows down to an idol every morning before coming to work. That managing director is no longer the man you are seeing but that idol and it should be dethroned. These days, fetish priests are fully employed by people who want protection. A very important man hired his own fetish priest to ensure that he retained his job. The fetish priest however, busied himself with good meals daily. Eventually, the man lost his position all the same.

5. **Diseases, demons and evil names:** You are to use the sword of deliverance against all diseases, demons, and every evil name; whether it is in this world or the world to come. When they finish mentioning the name of whatever they call, then you will say, I nullify it by the name which is above all names which is the name of Jesus, and the evil name will fizzle away. When the enemies start their incantations, do not worry. Once they finish, just say, "I annul everything you just said now, in the name of Jesus and of a surety, it gets annulled.

6.   The spirit of death: You are to use your sword of deliverance against the spirit of death and against all antagonistic spiritual beings.

7.   Possessed objects: You use your sword of deliverance against all possessed objects.

8.   The host of hell: You use your sword of deliverance against the host of hell because the enemy is restless, untiring and desperately wicked. If the enemy is not desperately wicked, how can somebody's head be removed and replaced with another one and the person goes about with that wrong identity? The person continues to fall out of favour because he or she is carrying about the wrong head.

The enemy fights with determination and firmness. The satanic world is much more disciplined than most churches. If you come late to satanic meetings, you could end up losing your firstborn as penalty. This is at variance with what happens when somebody comes late to church and shows no remorse.

The enemy will not give up anything unless he has to. He will not leave his victim unless he is forced out. They are ready to kill or do anything that will advance their own cause. They will use anything they can, they will take the form of anything available e.g crab, snake, lion, etc just to perpetrate their devilish acts. They can decide to appear as an angel of light. Their tactics are numerous. If you go to a prophet and find him carrying the skull of a human being, you may not be able to wait. Not many people will wait; they will run away. But they will not carry skulls, they will carry the Bible to deceive more people. Even if the fire on the Bible is burning their hands, they will try and endure it because they want to destroy somebody. They are working for a master who is ready to promote them when they destroy good people. They will pretend to be building but they are destroying. They do not mind giving people money if they can hand over their souls. At this juncture, I think you should close your eyes and pray this prayer with holy madness: "No demon will use my life for promotion, in the name of Jesus."

Sometime ago, we prayed for a girl to be delivered from powerful water spirits and she got delivered. After sometime, we found out that she was no longer zealous. When we asked her what the problem was, she said those spirits kept coming back to ask her what she has got since she accepted Jesus, that when she was with them, she had never had to ride in a commercial bus. Immediately she came out of her house, a Mercedes Benz car would be waiting to take her to wherever she was going but that now she trekked, rode in buses and sometimes did not even have money. "What's the use in serving God?" They asked her. She too was getting carried away not knowing that it is better to die a pauper and enter into life than for her to be very rich and go to hell.

Our enemies are very good traders. They specialize in spiritual bargains. They are ready to allow one or two demons to leave a person to convince him that the minister is powerful. A little bit of relief is permitted to allow the demons to gain more ground in the person's life. They can heal a person in order to win more people to hell fire. Somebody who has been blinded would say, "Well, I cannot leave this place because when I was poisoned and sick, they looked after me, because of that, I must show my allegiance, one should not be disloyal and ungrateful," whereas what they are doing is pampering the person to hell fire. Immediately you say you are going, they will say, "Remember, we are the ones that cured you." They know people that are totally powerless. It is a pity that among the most powerless are people who claim to come to church.

The first time the Lord showed me the meeting of witches and wizards, I noticed that three-quarters of them were women, while the remaining were men. They were rejoicing over people they had destroyed, things they had done, the confusion they had caused and they had somebody in the middle who did not know where he was, he was like a zombie. They had finished him. Only the carcass was walking about the streets. They know those who are totally powerless. They know those who can only read the Psalms. They know those who only pray in the church and never pray at home. They know those who fight and are very abusive. They know those whose tongues are their abode. It may surprise you to know that there are some demons living in the tongue just as there are some living in the head. Some people really need to pray very hard to deliver their tongues. They know who they can attack anytime, anywhere, anyhow and they know those they really have to sit down and plan before attacking because failure to do that might mean defeat for them.

As a Christian, you are supposed to have recognition in heaven and also in hell fire. Those demons said to the sons of Sceva, "Paul, we know, Jesus, we know, but who are you? Your names are not in our register of dangerous men. As far as we are concerned, you are our meat. How come you are insulting us, asking us to go out?" So, they dealt with them. Do you have recognition in hell fire? That is the question. They are prepared to make investment on a long term basis if their goal can be accomplished. They do not mind, they wait just as the devil waited for 80 years to get at Moses, and thereby prevented him from getting to the Promised Land. They can pursue a person for years. You have to be very careful because they have their agents scattered all over the place. I counsel women contractors to ensure that they do not first contract their bodies before they obtain contracts, or else the money will become the reward of iniquity and will not favour them in any way.

I know a woman who used to take her young beautiful daughter anywhere she went for contracts. One day, I asked her why she always took the girl along. She said, "That is the bait. When I get there and they see Funke, they're finished." Then I said, "Funke, let us pray." She said, "Excuse me sir, what kind of prayer?" I said, "We just want to pray." She then pleaded, "Sir, whatever you pray, please don't mention fire." She was afraid.

It is a misnomer to call prostitutes bush meat. It is the men who patronize them that should be called bush meat. The enemies of our souls know who is powerless. They ignore the command of powerless men. To even worsen it, they have sent so many people to sleep and they are busy sleeping. They like to work without being exposed, noticed or identified. Once you are able to see into their disguise, they will scream at you like they screamed at Jesus. How did they scream at Jesus? Luke 4: 33 -35 says,

> "And in the synagogue, there was a man, which had a spirit of an unclean devil, and cried out with a loud voice, saying, Let us alone; what have we to do with thee, thou Jesus of Nazareth? Art thou come to destroy us? I know thee who thou art; the Holy One of God. And Jesus rebuked him, saying, Hold thy peace, and come out of him."

We can see that Jesus was never gentle with evil spirits.

CHAPTER 5

WHY WE MUST NOT LEAVE

UNCLEAN SPIRITS ALONE

WHY WE MUST NOT LEAVE UNCLEAN SPIRITS ALONE

1. They want believers to stop praying against them and this is why people are attacking ministries where they do spiritual warfare. All they are saying is, "These people, leave us alone." But if you leave them alone, they will operate unmolested and unhindered in many lives.

2. We must not leave them alone because we can never lose. The Bible says, "Greater is He that is in you than he that is in the world" (1 John4:4). We are more than conquerors that is why we must not leave them alone.

3. We must not leave them alone because we have received a commandment that we should fight and we must fight. It is not a suggestion. It is a commandment, a marching order which we must carry out.

4. We must not leave them alone because without resistance, the enemy will not flee. The Bible says, **"Resist the devil and he will flee"** (James 4:7). If you do not resist him, he will not flee.

5. We must not leave them alone because if we run away from the battle, we are finished. If you say, "I want to backslide," you are finished because they will shoot you at the back so that you cannot run away. Even if you insist on running, where are you running to? Back to occultists? If you run away, you shall be treated as a rebel.

   There was war somewhere and the soldiers who were tired of the war and wanted to go devised a trick of discharging themselves. They would shoot themselves in the legs and the authorities would dismiss them as "wounded' and they would go back home. They were doing that quite successfully until they brought in a tough commander. For the first person who did it, the commander moved close to his leg and said, "This is not an enemy's shot, otherwise the area will not be so dark. You shot yourself because you do not want to fight again therefore, let me finish the job for you." He shot him dead and said, "Anyone who wants to shoot himself is free to do so," and the trick promptly stopped. They stayed, fought and won. As Christians, we cannot run or retreat.

6. We must not leave them alone because winners do not quit.

7. We must not leave them alone because that will mean that we have refused to acknowledge the kingdom of God.

SHADOW PROBLEMS

One day, a little child was fascinated by his own shadow. He looked at the shadow on the wall and got excited. He found that as he moved, the shadow moved, when he bowed down, the shadow too bowed down. He found that sometimes, the shadow would get bigger and then get smaller again. The boy spent about thirty minutes playing with this shadow. He said to himself, "This thing must be a friend because anything I do, he does." He then decided to hold his hand but found that he could not hold it. He was shocked. He tried holding the leg, the feet, etc, but failed. So, he started running away from the shadow. Then he was amazed to see the shadow following him then he started screaming. There are some shadow problems, anywhere you go, they follow you. When you bow, they bow. When you rise they rise. When you sit down, they sit down. I want you to pray with holy madness like this: "All shadow problems, I cut you off now, in the name of Jesus.

Beloved, you can see that this message is for those who love Jesus and hate the devil. It is for those who hate bondage but love freedom. I am sure you would like to handle the sword of deliverance and put it into effective use. But to do this, there are certain things you need to have.

CHAPTER 6

QUALIFICATIONS NEEDED TO HANDLE THE

SWORD of DELIVERANCE

QUALIFICATIONS NEEDED
TO HANDLE THE
SWORD OF DELIVERANCE

I am sure you would like to handle the sword of deliverance and put it into effective use. But to do this, there are certain things you need to have:

1. NEW BIRTH: The first major qualification needed is a new birth. You must be born-again and this is not negotiable. This is where most people miss out. Anybody who is not born-again, as far as the Bible is concerned is not a Christian. He may be going to church but he is not a Christian. Standing at the abattoir does not make you a cow. You may be a priest, pastor, general overseer, general superintendent, general secretary of whatever, if you are not born-again, you are not a Christian. That is the stand of the Bible.

John 3: 3-5 says:

> "Jesus answered and said unto him, Verily, verily, I say unto thee; except a man be born again, he cannot see the kingdom of God. Nicodemus saith unto him, How can a man be born when he is old? Can he enter the second time into his mother's womb and be born? Jesus answered, Verily, verily, I say unto thee, except a man be born of water and of the Spirit, he cannot enter into the kingdom of God."

This is a very clear statement that needs no argument at all. Become born-again and have the ticket to heaven or refuse to become born again and perish. It does not matter whether you are the chairman of any committee of any church, or if you are the one that helped them build the greatest cathedral in the country, you may do all that and still not be born-again. You may have degrees in Bible studies and still be a sinner.

To be born-again means to be born from above;

begotten from above and once you are born from above, the Bible says, you cannot commit sin. If you do, it must be accidental. But how many people today can say that their sins are mistakes? Are there not some people, who premeditate on sins and carry them out?

The stand of the Bible is that the Lord winks at the time of ignorance but for willful sin, the Bible says, "though hand join in hand, no sinner will go unpunished." So, if you are born-again, sin will not become your habit. That is why this terminology has to be well-defined for you to know and understand it.

If you say you are born-again, how did it happen? How did you meet the Lord? Was it during a message or prayer or you just completed the back of an American tract? Or you shook the hand of a bishop and declared that you are born-again. Being born-again is a complete transformation. In the old days, in Pentecostal churches, those who wanted to get born-again, came to the altar to pray.

They prayed themselves through to salvation because this is very important. Once you are saved, your name is written in the Book of Life, that is when you can say you are born-again.

The greatest headache in the church today is that those who are not born-again and speaking in tongues are not doing the business of God. That is why in the Bible arrangement of spiritual gifts, the first one mentioned is, "In my name, they shall cast out devils," before "They shall speak with new tongues." But today, people have turned it upside down. When somebody who is not delivered and born-again is speaking in tongues, problem happens.

IMPORTANCE OF NEW BIRTH

Why is this new birth important in handling the sword of deliverance? According to I Corinthians 12:13, every born-again believer is a member of the body of Christ and that body is not polluted. Every born-again Christian is a member of the family of God in heaven and on earth. According to Ephesians 3:15, every born-again Christian is a son or daughter of God.

John 1:12 says:

" But as many as received him, to them gave he power to become the sons of God, even to them that believe on his name. "

Every born-again Christian belongs to the Lord by adoption. According to Ephesians 1: 5, every born-again Christian has been cleansed by the blood of Jesus and has been forgiven, redeemed or bought back from the slave market of sin and set free through the precious blood of Jesus. Born-again Christians have been reconciled and regenerated. They have been accepted and are citizens of heaven.

There is a level you get to with God and your problem will not be temptation harassing you because you would be immune to temptation. If temptation is still your problem as a child of God, check your salvation.

All born-again Christians have been elected and called to be holy persons. They are already seated in heavenly places with Christ. Jesus calls them the salt of the earth and the light of the world. He says, they have everlasting life. He calls them His sheep. The Bible calls them saints, the temple of God and the temple of the Holy Ghost. They are free from condemnation. They are partakers of God's grace and are called unto the fellowship of the Son of God.

It is not a light thing to say, "I am born again." The Bible calls it a new creation or an ambassador of Christ. Born-again Christians are the children of light. They have been delivered from the powers of darkness, unto the Kingdom of the dear Son of God and the Bible then calls them kings.

The fact that somebody is ignorant about a thing does not mean that the thing cannot affect him. For example, if you are ignorant about the eye disease called conjunctivitis and you use your hand to rub the eyes of somebody who is infected and use the same hand to rub your own eyes, you will become infected too. Ignorance is no immunity. You must be born-again before you can enjoy the benefits of salvation.

2. YOU MUST BE FREE FROM BONDAGE: You cannot use the sword successfully when your hands are tied. Right from the womb, a lot of people have been in bondage because of who they are. A lot of people are in bondage because of certain things they have done which they are not supposed to have done. Many people are in bondage because of certain places they have visited that they ought not to have gone. Many people are in bondage because external enemies are fighting them day and night. Many people too are in bondage because of what people have done to them. When these kinds of things are in place in a person's life, effective use of the sword would be impossible.

3. YOU MUST WIN THE BATTLE OF THE MIND: Sometime ago, I read two news items that got me thinking. The first one was titled, "Girl sets herself on fire." When I read the details, I discovered that a certain girl set herself ablaze because she was jilted by a man who had promised to marry her. The second day, I read in yet another paper a news item titled, "Man drinks acid." After reading these news items, a lot of things went through my mind and I started asking myself what was going on in the minds of these two people that made them to do these terrible things to themselves. For somebody to decide to do such things, the mind must have been bombarded by some forces. What was that force that was ruling the minds of these people to the extent that they decided to take their own lives. The Bible says that the human mind is very delicate and that there are so many things that can render the mind of a man unsound. Otherwise, the Bible will not say, "For God has not given us the spirit of fear; but of power, of love and of a sound mind." If the Bible is talking about sound mind, it means there are many people with unsound minds.

Many things can render a man's mind unsound. I will tell you some of them so that you can know how to win the battle of the mind.

a. Bad health: This can set a man thinking horrible things, and the devil has a way of magnifying things for people. A minor ailment could be so expanded as to put an affected person in trouble. Before you finish telling the person that the ailment is not as serious as it looks, the devil would have given the person lectures on the number of people the disease had killed thereby causing the person to start evil meditation. In his subtle way, the devil will not mention thousands and thousands of people that have received healing by prayer, but will mention one or two that died after they were prayed for.

Evil thoughts can render the mind unsound. For some people, the bad thoughts get to such a level that they suffocate the word of God in their hearts. Such people cannot use the sword of the Spirit.

b. Evil inheritance: A common case is the spirit of worry. It is possible for both daddy and mummy to be worry bags and eventually transfer the spirit to their offspring. A statement such as, "Like father like son," then becomes apt.

c. Lack of use: A mind kept busy with reading the Scriptures and memorising things will function adequately. But when a mind is kept out of use, it will be rendered unsound.

That popular 2 Timothy 1: 7 says:

"For God has not given us the spirit of fear, but of power, of love and of a sound mind."

So, the first question I would like to ask you is, "Is your mind sound?" The number one vagabond is the mind. It can wander all over the place. It is possible that as you are reading this book your mind has travelled to a far place. It is possible for you to be thinking about your wares or what you will eat.

The mind likes to wander if it is not controlled. But as a Christian, you must deal with the gate crashers and intruders coming into your mind. If you let them in, then there will be problem. This is a serious issue and it is a major area of defeat for many. When God wants to start working in a person's life, He starts from the mind. When the devil too wants to manipulate a person, he starts from the same place. You must win that battle. It does not make any sense if you teach a soldier how to shoot a gun, give him a gun and send him to the warfront, and by the time he gets there, he is busy thinking about his wife at home instead of concentrating on the war. Certainly, he will fail. Although he has the weapon, his state of mind will render the weapon useless.

HOW DO WE GET OVER THE PROBLEM OF UNSOUND MIND?

i. Embrace the fact that a sound mind is your birthright as a Christian. It is part of your inheritance and you must claim it. Do not start saying, "Well, I am just being human." God knows that you are neither a goat nor a stick before He says a sound mind belongs to you. So, embrace that fact that a sound mind is your lot.

ii. Submit your mind to God's word and to the Holy Spirit. It is important for you to do that. Renew your mind with the word of God always. Do not read the Bible like a story book. Read it to feed your spirit and regularly too.

iii. Refuse to let your thoughts go on rampage like undisciplined children.

Understand that you have the right to decide what to think about. You have the right to throw out any useless thought from your heart. You have the right to be the immigration officer at the door of your heart, and decide what enters. So, bring the discipline of God into your thinking. Decide that your thoughts must act only under your jurisdiction. Many people's thoughts are wayward, out of control, immoral and doubtful. This makes it impossible for them to handle the sword of deliverance. When you handle the sword and your mind is undisciplined, the enemy can see it.

I remember a student crusade we had a long time ago. On the last day of the crusade, we were ready to go to the villages for evangelism. But shortly before we left, we reminded the students that there would be confrontations by the villagers who might bring out their talking idols and ask them to make their Jesus to do the same thing. And that anyone who was afraid could stay behind to intercede for those that would go. As expected, out of the initial 2000 people that signified their intention to go, only 57 made it.

Defeat comes from the mind. If your mind tells you that you are a poor man, you remain poor. If your mind tells you that you will be healed, it shall be so. But immediately you allow it to be wandering aimlessly, trouble then comes.

The mind is where the picture of evil things are taken. It is where the evil negative is developed. Once it is cancelled at that level, things will begin to work. Decide to be the immigration officer at the gateway of your mind.

GATEWAYS TO THE MIND

There are several gateways to the mind.

A. THE EYE GATE: Make a covenant with your eyes not to look at what you should not look at. If you are a television addict, your eyes need deliverance.

Somebody did a simple research. He got about fifty families in Europe and offered thirty of them money if they would refuse to watch television for one month. Then he allowed the remaining twenty to watch television. He later found that the 30 families that were not allowed to watch television fell ill. It was as if a powerful drug they were used to was withdrawn from them. Televison is modern-day witchcraft because it is everywhere and takes most prayer time away from people. I do not say you should throw away your TV set or break it. But what I am saying is this, it is easy for you to make an idol of something you bought and it is easy for you to be in bondage of something you purchased. That is what we call, "Purchased bondage."

B. EAR GATE: The mind has another gate called, the "ear gate." What do you listen to? Do you listen to gossips? The reason we have gossips is that we have listening ears too. If your ears have received deliverance, when somebody says, "Did you hear what so-and-so person said about you?" You will say, "Ok, can you repeat what you just said before this person?" If he says no, then he needs deliverance. The ear gate pollutes the mind.

C. MEMORY GATE: A lot of people just sit down and daydream. They also have flashbacks of the things which the Lord has removed from their memories. It is rather tragic for a born-again child of God to lie down on his bed and start recollecting all the immoral acts he was involved in right from his primary school days.

D. THE HABIT GATE: It is possible for someone to continuously do something even when he knows that it is bad. So, make up your mind that only those thoughts that carry divine passports will be allowed to move into your mind. It is a personal decision.

E. STRONGHOLDS: Pull down the stronghold which the enemy might have established in your mind. A lot of minds have strongholds already built in them, which must be brought down no matter how hard.

F. THE OLD NATURE: Refuse to allow your mind to go back to the old nature. When it wants to go back to what you used to think of as an unbeliever, aggressively address it to go back to its resting place, in the way of the Psalmist.

G. OPEN A BANK ACCOUNT OF QUALITY THOUGHTS:

Phillipians 4: 8 says,

> " *Finally, brethren, whatsoever things are true, whatsoever things are honest, whatsoever things are just; whatsoever things are pure, whatsoever things are lovely, whatsoever things are of good report, if there be any virtue, if there be any praise, think on these things.* "

These are the kinds of thoughts the Bible wants us to fill our minds with. Let there be an endless supply of wholesome and nourishing materials into your heart. I am explaining this in detail because this is where defeat comes from. Some people get defeated right from their beds in the morning. Do not forget, the devil is an early riser.

THE SWORD OF DELIVERANCE

H. FEED YOUR MIND ON THE WORD OF

GOD: Otherwise, the devil will feed it with his thoughts. An average Christian who has been born again for two years should know a minimum of fifty-two memory verses. It is therefore profitable to begin a programme of regular Bible study. Meditate on the Scriptures. Learn the Scriptures by heart. This is how to keep your mind on the word of God and ward off satan.

I.   REFUSE TO GIVE WAY TO ANXIETY, WORRY OR DEPRESSION.

You must win the battle of the mind to correctly handle the sword of deliverance.

4. PREPARE FOR WAR: The next qualification for handling the sword of deliverance is to prepare for war. In warfare, the first thing to do is to be trained. How do you prepare as a Christian soldier? The Bible tells us how to prepare in Ephesians 6:10-11. It says:

❝ *"Finally, my brethren, be strong in the Lord, and in the power of his might. Put on the whole armour of God, that ye may be able to stand against the wiles of the devil."* ❞

HOW TO PREPARE FOR WAR

1. Put on your spiritual armour: To successfully destroy the works of satan, you must first of all be able to stand against his attacks. All your defensive armour has to be in place before you seize the sword and go out. We are to allow the devil no place in our lives.

2. Know your weapons:

Ephesians 6: 12-18 says:

❝ *For we wrestle not against flesh and blood, but against principalities, against powers, against the rulers of the darkness of this world, against spiritual wickedness in high places. Wherefore take unto you the whole armour of God,*

71

> *that ye may be able to withstand in the evil day, and having done all, to stand. Stand therefore, having your loins girt about with truth, and having on the breastplate of righteousness. And your feet shod with the preparation of the gospel of peace. Above all, taking the shield of faith, wherewith ye shall be able to quench all the fiery darts of the wicked. And take the helmet of salvation, and the sword of the Spirit, which is the word of God. Praying always with all prayer and supplication in the Spirit, and watching thereunto with all perseverance and supplication for all saints.*

Each piece of the armour represents a specific truth. Put that truth on by walking in the truth. So, if as a Christian, the attack of the enemy prospers in your life, the first question you should ask yourself is, 'Is my armour on?' The Bible says, "Touch not my anointed, do my prophets no harm." But if an anointed is being touched or a prophet is being harmed, then a thorough self-examination is necessary.

3. Train for battle: The Bible says we should take the sword of the Spirit which is the Word of God. This implies that you must know your Bible by regular reading and thorough digestion of the word. Let it become part and parcel of your life. When you have done all, then you are protected. Realise also that at the battlefront, you cannot afford to look back, for the arrows of the enemy will hit you. You must know how to apply the blood of the Lamb as part of your training. Revelation 12: 11 says:

66 *And they overcame him by the blood of the Lamb, and by the word of their testimony...* 99

You must know about the power of the Holy Spirit. Acts 1:8 says,

66 *But ye shall receive power, after that the Holy Ghost is come upon you...* 99

You must know the ministry of prayer. You must also know the ministry of praise and thanksgiving. You must know the ministry of the word of our testimony. When somebody testifies to what God has done, he defeats the enemy. When you run away from the testimony, you strengthen the enemy more to fight you. You must know the fire of God. Hebrews 12:29 says,

66 *For our God is a consuming fire.* 99

You must know about the angels of the living God, who are ready to fight for you. These are our weapons.

4. Know your adversary: We are fighting the devil who has very wicked intelligence. This must be borne in mind.

5. Overcome the flesh: This is where the greatest problem comes from. You must learn to listen to the voice of the Holy Spirit at all times. This is a sure way of destroying the flesh. It is only then that reading of the Bible is done with ease. Your life as a Christian will not be productive until you "die." It is very sad that many times, we fail to recognise our battle-ground. You cannot cast out the flesh. Many abound, who instead of disciplining themselves and praying to be crucified, they believe all they need is deliverance. You cannot deliver the flesh, it has to be crucified. If it is a demon, the demon can be cast out.

Beloved, you must learn these principles to be able to use the sword of deliverance. Many believers are carrying the sword but cannot effectively use it because they lack the knowledge of these principles. It is an offence to be an ineffective soldier. It is an offence too to doubt God. If you are not putting on your whole armour, you cannot handle the sword of deliverance. That is why the song writer says, "Christians seek not yet repose, hear thy guardian angel say, thou art in the midst of foes, watch and pray." It says, "Put your whole armour on; put it on day and night and ambush lies the evil one, watch and pray." We therefore need to pray.

This is why many people are being defeated in their dreams. Countless number of Christians are being suffocated on their beds. Many Christian sisters are sexually harassed in the dream. Many people are pursued by masquerades and other agents of the devil in their dreams. Why are they not able to resist them? Why are they not able to turn the table around in those dreams? It is all because they cannot handle the sword of deliverance. You need to cry out to the Lord for His assistance to enable you meet all these conditions and become an effective soldier, a soldier who is battle-ready always and sure of victory, and you will be victorious, in Jesus' name.

PRAYER POINTS

1. Let every attack against my spiritual life be frustrated, in the name of Jesus.

2. I command the spirit of harassment to leave now, in the name of Jesus.

3. I command the spirit of judgment to depart now, in the name of Jesus.

4. O Lord, speak soundness into my mind and body, in Jesus' name.

5. Every witch delegated against me, receive the sword of fire, in the name of Jesus.

6. I reverse every witchcraft curse issued against me, in the name of Jesus.

7. I condemn all the evil spirits condemning me, in the name of Jesus.

8. Let the sword of fire pursue my oppressors into the Red Sea, in Jesus' name.

9. Let the sword of Jehovah render vengeance to my enemies, in the name of Jesus.

10. Powers raging to frustrate my destiny, die, in the name of Jesus.

11. Powers extending the mystery of iniquity of my

father's house, die, in the name of Jesus.

12. Marine bankers, forest bankers and rock bankers in my foundation, release my virtues, in the name of Jesus.

13. Glory killers assigned against me, die, in the name of Jesus.

14. Masquerading enemies, hear the word of the Lord, destroy yourselves, in the name of Jesus.

15. The enemy will not laugh me to scorn by the power in the blood of Jesus, in th name of Jesus.

16. Holy Ghost fire, destroy my oppressors, in the name of Jesus.

17. Serpents and scorpions from my foundation, die, in the name of Jesus.

18. Inherited warfare, die, in the name of Jesus.

19. Collective warfare, die, in the name of Jesus.

20. Poison of darkness in my body, die, in the name of Jesus.

YORUBA PUBLICATIONS
1. Adura Agbayori
2. Adura Ti Nsi Oke Ni Dii
3. Ojo Adura

FRENCH PUBLICATIONS
1. Pluie De Prière
2. Esprit De Vagabondage
3. En Finir Avec Les Forces Maléfiques De La Maison De Ton Père
4. Que L'envoutement Périsse
5. Frappez L'adversaire et il Fuira
6. Comment Recevoir La Délivrance Du Mari Et De La Femme De Nuit
7. Comment Se Délivrer Soimeme
8. Pouvoir Contre Les Terroristes Spirituels
9. Prières De Percées Pour Les Homes D'affaires
10. Prier Jusqu'a Remporter La Victoire
11. Prières Violentes Pour Humilier Les Problèmes Opiniâtres
12. Prière Pour Détruire Les Maladies Et Les Infirmités
13. Le Combat Spiritual Et Le Foyer
14. Bilan Spirituel Personnel
15. Victories Sur Les Rêves Sataniques
16. Prier De Combat Contre 70 Esprits Déchaînés
17. La Déviation Satanique De La Race Noire
18. Ton Combat Et Ta Stratégie
19. Votre Fondement Et Votre Destin
20. Révoquer Les Décrets Maléfiques

21. Cantique Des Cantiques
22. Le Mauvais Cri Des Idoles
23. Quand Les Choses Deviennent Difficiles
24. Les Stratégies De Prier Pour Les Célibataires
25. Se Libérer Des Alliances Maléfiques
26. Démanteler La Sorcellerie
27. La Délivrance: Le Flacon De Médicament De Dieu
28. La Délivrance De La Tête
29. Commander Le Matin
30. Ne Grand Mais Lie
31. Pouvoir Contre Les Demons Tropicaux
32. Le Programme De Transfert Des Richesse
33. Les étudiants à l'école De La Peur
34. L'étoile Dans Votre Ciel
35. Les Saisons De La Vie
36. Femme Tu Es Libérée

ANNUAL 70 DAYS PRAYER AND FASTING PUBLICATIONS

1. Prayers That Bring Miracles
2. Let God Answer By Fire
3. Prayers To Mount Up With Wings As Eagles
4. Prayers That Bring Explosive Increase
5. Prayers For Open Heavens
6. Prayers To You Fulfill Your Divine Destiny
7. Prayers That Make God To Answer And Fight By Fire
8. Prayers That Bring Unchallengeable Victory And Breakthrough Rainfall Bombardments

9. Prayers That Bring Dominion Prosperity And
    Uncommon Success
10. Prayers That Bring Power And Overflowing Progress
11. Prayers That Bring Laughter And Enlargement
    Breakthroughs
12. Prayers That Bring Uncommon Favour And
    Breakthroughs
13. Prayers That Bring Unprecedented Greatness &
    Unmatchable Increase
14. Prayers That Bring Awesome Testimonies And
    Turnaround Breakthroughs

ABOUT THE BOOK

Many believers are defeated everyday in the battles of life. Many brothers and sisters are sexually harassed in the dream and many are being pursued by masquerades and other satanic agents in their dreams. And as a result, life has become hell on earth for them although they are Christians. They have become pawns in the hands of the enemy because they cannot handle the sword of deliverance.

This book reveals to you how you can possess and handle the sword of deliverance effectively and come out victorious in the battles of life.

ABOUT THE AUTHOR

Dr. D. K. Olukoya is the General Overseer of the Mountain of Fire and Miracles Ministries and The Battle Cry Christian Ministries.

The Mountain of Fire and Miracles Ministries' Headquarters is the largest single Christian congregation in Africa with attendance of over 120,000 in single meetings.

MFM is a full gospel ministry devoted to the revival of Apostolic signs, Holy Ghost Fireworks, miracles and the unlimited demonstration of the power of God to deliver to the uttermost. Absolute holiness within and without as spiritual insecticide and pre-requisite for heaven is openly taught. MFM is a do-it-yourself Gospel Ministry, where your hands are trained to wage war and your fingers to do battle.

Dr. Olukoya holds a First Class Honours degree in Micro-Biology from the University of Lagos and a PhD in Molecular Genetics from the University of Reading, United Kingdom. As a researcher, he has over seventy scientific publications to his credit.

Anointed by God, Dr. Olukoya is a prophet, evangelist, teacher and preacher of the Word. His life and that of his wife, Shade and their son Elijah Toluwani are living proofs that all power belongs to God.

978-978-49173-9-1

www.ingramcontent.com/pod-product-compliance
Lightning Source LLC
Chambersburg PA
CBHW060133050426
42448CB00010B/2105

* 9 7 8 0 6 9 2 4 8 9 2 1 5 *